THE
DOORKEEPER

THE
DOORKEEPER

BECOME THE HUSBAND AND FATHER GOD WANTS YOU TO BE

SONNY GUESS

Formatting and cover design by Anne McLaughlin, Blue Lake Design
Published in the United States by Baxter Press, Friendswood, Texas

ISBN: 978-1-888237-67-2

Eleventh Printing

To Delores,
the one who kept loving me even when
I wasn't the Doorkeeper of our home.

Table of Contents

Acknowledgements

First and above all, I thank my Lord Jesus Christ for my salvation, and I thank the precious Holy Spirit for giving me the message of this book.

To Delores, my loving and supportive bride, thank you for the long hours you spent by yourself in prayer while I was writing. I love you for being a great example of the loving bride every man truly desires.

To my children David and Denene, Michael and Trish, Lisa and Dave, thank you for your loving and prayerful support during the process of writing this book. I love you.

To my beautiful grandchildren, Brittany, Dakotah, Mackenzie, Tyler, Coby, Madison, Caleb, Zachary, thanks for the wonderful and fun memories. You have blessed me through laughter and love with some of the greatest moments a grandfather could have experienced. I love you.

To my daughter Lisa Wilbanks, for the great sacrifice of editing this book and spending long hours even when you were really sick and didn't feel like doing it. You used your gifts and talents to keep dad's grammar straight, and you made sure the book was written correctly. I love you.

To my wonderful mother, Marguerite Guess, words can't express the blessing of being raised by a godly mother. I've always known my prayer warrior was in the background, rejoicing as God blessed and praying as Satan interfered. I love you, Mom.

To my mother-in-law, Rose Mary Raney, thanks for never forgetting to pray for this ministry and continuing to be a great spokesperson for your son-in-law. I love you, Rosie.

To Mona Bjornson, thank you for taking pictures, being sure they were in the right format, and always encouraging me when I became discouraged.

To our Sunday School class, for all the hugs, cards, calls, and true Christian love shown to me during this time. Your prayers helped me to finish the task that God called me to do.

To Amy Burgess, thank you for getting the pictures of Greg and Sally Sue and their children for the cover of the book. What a blessing to have someone who took this challenge to be a spiritual project for God.

To all the ones who have shared testimonies, thanks for sharing some difficult times in your life and praising God as you watched Him intervene in every situation. God bless you!

To the Greg Sipe family, thank you for spending your time to allow us to photo you as you prayed for your children to become men and women of God.

To Pat Springle at Baxter Press, I'm thankful God sent me to you. Your spiritual insights and help in all areas of this book really improved its quality for the glory of God! I love you, brother.

To Greg and Sally Sue Harriss, thank you for allowing me to take pictures of your beautiful family for the cover of this book. Greg, you have certainly been a role model of the spiritual Doorkeeper, and I pray other young men will follow your example. I love ya'll.

INTRODUCTION

The Necessity of Being the Doorkeeper

I was born in a family in which my mother was a strong Christian. I accepted the Lord on June 25, 1954, at the age of nine, and the Lord began immediately changing my life. I was a youth leader through high school, and the Lord began to prepare me for a special time in His ministry.

On January 8, 1965, I married Delores Raney. We were blessed with three beautiful children: David (June 9, 1967), Michael (August 27, 1968), and Lisa (June 25, 1970). My wife stayed home with our children during their earlier years. It was the thrill of my life to come home and to have our babies cleaned up, smelling good with baby oil and standing at the front screen door, jumping up and down saying, "Daddy's home! Daddy's home!" While I loved on my babies, my bride would put a great meal on the table and later call us to supper. We laughed and enjoyed mom's good cooking, and I remember thinking to myself, *Life can't be much better than this!*

In 1972 God called us into the music ministry. I then began a life of great joy serving my Lord through music. We've had the privilege of serving in several churches in Texas and Florida, but in 1978 God changed my ministry. I became the City Business Administrator in the beautiful East Texas town of Winnsboro.

Our children attended church regularly, and we thought that their involvement in the youth group would be all they needed to become good Christian leaders one day. As their teenage years came along, however, our family experienced more and more conflicts, and I could see that my children were heading away from God. The television programs they were watching depicted and contained language that was not to my liking, but, like most other Christian families in our church, I chose to ignore them. Before long, all this ungodliness became "normal," and I ignored it completely. After all, I was a busy man keeping up my reputation up in the community, teaching a large Sunday school class, and praying that my kids wouldn't mess up so I wouldn't be embarrassed in the community.

As time passed, we experienced the heartache of a rebellious child and a child who attempted suicide. At this point of need, my heart finally turned toward one of the most neglected things in my life . . . **my family.** As God spoke to my heart about what I was to do, my faithful wife agreed that we should rise early and pray together over our children to ask God for wisdom to deal with what now seemed an impossible task of turning our teenagers back to God. As the Lord graciously worked, I learned that He is faithful. Nothing is impossible with Him!

As you read this book, I pray that the power of the precious Holy Spirit will enlighten you and strengthen your family as I share how God taught me to fulfill the most important role that the man has in his home—the spiritual Doorkeeper.

The door of a house is the place where people come in for security and go out for adventure. God has called men to be the Doorkeepers of our homes, to provide safety and protection against the physical and spiritual attacks of the world, and to be a launching pad for our children to follow the Lord for the rest of their lives. Becoming the Doorkeeper God wants us to be is the highest call for a man today. In this book, I want to share the life-changing principles I've learned by the grace of God. Above the title of each chapter, you'll find an image of a door with a key in the lock. Each of us holds the key to our family's future. This is a solemn responsibility and an awesome privilege. I hope we all are honest about our failures so we will turn to God and trust him to change us. No matter how hard that choice may be, I assure you that it's worth it.

This book can be used in many different ways. First, you may choose to use it as a personal guide of instruction to become the Doorkeeper of your home. I encourage you to take time to answer the questions at the end of each chapter.

Reflecting on these important topics will help you apply God's truth to your thoughts, attitudes, and choices. Secondly, you may choose to get two or three men to meet on a regular basis and complete the study together. Thirdly, your church's men's ministry can use this as a several week study. No matter which way you choose, accountability is the key. Have at least yourself and another man who will commit to having regular discussions at a weekly breakfast or another chosen time. May God bless you as you begin your Doorkeeper journey!

When God Said,
"Write It Down!"

In June of 2004, I received a call asking me to be a keynote speaker at the annual men's conference at East Paris Baptist Church in Paris, Texas. I asked what would be involved, and my great friend Dr. Chick Holland shared with me that they would have four keynote speakers who would be speaking at various times during the two-day conference, and they like to use laymen to speak. They also used great men of God who had been educated in the Word and were being used mightily of God. I looked at the brochure and I saw that an awesome man named Dr. Ergun Caner, professor of theology and church history, at Liberty University was a keynote speaker. He is a nationally known conference speaker and author. Next, there was Dr. Jeff Crawford, dean of Shiloh Christian School in Springdale, Arkansas. The third speaker was a well-known and respected judge, The Honorable Judge Robert Newsom, District Judge, Sulphur Springs, Texas. Finally, there was me, a Christian layman, sportsman, harmonica player, and a member of Christian Bowhunters of America. To say the least, I was totally intimidated by the lineup of great speakers.

As the conference approached, I stayed before the Lord on a daily basis looking to Him for guidance, but I still didn't have a sense of direction. One day out of desperation, I cried out, "Lord, what would you have me say?" His precious Holy Spirit spoke to me and told me to get a pencil and paper and write down what He was going to tell me. I quickly obeyed. The Holy Spirit began to remind me that what I had learned with my teenage children was how to be the Doorkeeper of my home. That was the message He wanted me to share.

As the Lord brought to mind the good and the ugly things that happened in my home, He also reminded me of the power of God's Holy Spirit and His role in seeing that my family had been brought back together under God. He told me to open my mouth and He would fill it with God's Word and God's way. As I began to write, it was almost as if I couldn't keep up. I was writing the thoughts that the Holy Spirit was giving me as fast as I could. Family stories flooded my mind. Passages of Scripture that I had learned as a child also came back to me. God's promises confirmed the miracle of love and grace that brought my family back together. But miraculous transformation isn't just for me and my family. This miracle is available for every believer who chooses to accept it and act upon His Word.

The Holy Spirit assured me that day, "Share your life story of how I showed you how to become the Doorkeeper of your home, and I'll do the rest." In the remaining chapters of this book, I'll do just that. As you read the remainder of this book, remember: What God has done for me, He stands willing to do for you and your family. The theme of the conference was Joshua 24:15 which reads, "Choose you this day whom you will serve." The choice will be yours. I pray that you will be prayed up and ready to receive instructions as the Holy Spirit gives them to you through the reading of this book. To God be the glory!

Following the questions at the end of each chapter, I've included a section we're calling "My Perspective." Many people—both men and women—have written to me to express their heart-felt convictions about the role of the Doorkeeper, and my publisher wanted to include some of these letters and emails in the book to show how God is using these principles to transform men's lives. I hope you enjoy reading them.

"Choose you this day whom you will serve."

—Joshua 24:15

PERSONAL SPIRITUAL INSIGHTS

1. Look back at the Introduction. What are some ways I failed as a father? Can you relate to any of them? Explain your answer.

2. In this chapter, I describe how the Holy Spirit spoke to me to give me direction. What are some ways the Holy Spirit "speaks" to us?

3. God did a genuine miracle of restoration in my family. Do you believe He wants to work powerfully in your life and your relationships with your wife and children? Write down the miracles you would like to see happen in your family.

4. As you read this book and examine your home, you should be prayed up and ready to receive instructions as the Holy Spirit gives them to you. Write your prayer below of changes you desire to see in your home.

My perspective...

Robin Coe

Thank you hardly seems enough to express what your ministry has meant to me! I have been so burdened for the young husbands and fathers in our churches. Many of them are Christians, but they don't know what to do for their families. The absence of spiritual leadership is ultimately weakening our entire church body. When the head is wounded, it's hard for the body to function as it should.

Our children, and especially our sons, are young now, but they are watching. They need strong leadership modeled, but I honestly don't think my generation knows where to begin.

I plugged in your message on a long family trip in the car and wanted to shout for joy! Your words are exactly what we needed to hear! Our men need permission to matter for the Kingdom. Your words give them the keys to the gate so they are able to keep it! How I pray each man hears what you said and begins to stand in the void that has been filled till now only by the prayers of their women. I'm longing for the truth of your words to pierce and to change each heart!

You and Delores are such a blessing! Your shining faces in worship tell me so clearly that not only do you know Him—you adore Him! There are only a handful like you on any given Sunday. I see people who are distracted, restless, bored, irritated, and weighed down by church politics, but very few are in His presence. Thank you for your example and your testimony! May God bless you richly for all you do for His work in this world!

Becoming God's Spiritual Doorkeeper

Delores and I went on a trip to Florida with three of our eight grandchildren. We had our two oldest granddaughters, Brittany and Dakotah, and Tyler, our oldest grandson. Tyler was five years old and the youngest of the three. As we were traveling home on I-10 through the Florida panhandle, Tyler hollered from the back of the suburban that he had to go to the bathroom. Now, Gran was driving, and she goes the speed limit. No emergency will make her go any faster. I asked Tyler, "Number one or number two?" He said, "Number two." I knew at that point that we were in "Emergency Mode," but Gran had that cruise control set on the speed limit, and that's as fast as we would be going. I saw the road sign: "Next exit 23 miles." Now I knew we were in trouble! We encouraged Tyler to hang in there, but he was moaning and groaning in the back seat. We finally reached the exit, and there was a McDonald's in sight. I exclaimed, "Praise God for those golden arches!" When I finally got him into the bathroom and pulled his little pants down, he had already gone some. He looked down and then looked back at me and said, "Pops, I was afraid of that!" I said, "I was afraid of that too, Tyler."

As I began to laugh at Tyler's wit, the Holy Spirit spoke to me and said, "This is what's happening in homes across the country." God gave me a spiritual lesson from this story. You see, our children are crying out for spiritual love and attention. We hear the moanings and groanings, but we choose to overlook them, hoping their problems will go away. Then something big happens that destroys our home and our family, and we say, "Oh man, I was afraid that would happen." Why did it happen? It happened because we weren't strong as a husband and father. We weren't the Doorkeepers of our homes!

In John 10:2-3, we read, "To him the doorkeeper openeth." I submit to you that it's your job as a husband and father to be the Doorkeeper of your family. It's not your wife's job, not your child's, and not your parents'. Sometimes, we men leave all the upbringing, discipline, and problems of the home to our wives. I believe God has a favorite word for that: "Baloney!" As men, it's our spiritual job to be that Doorkeeper. Our responsibility is to keep God in our homes—and keep Satan out.

In II Peter 2:19-20, the Word says, "For of whom a man is overcome, of the same is he brought in bondage. For if after they have escaped the pollutions of the world through the knowledge of the Lord and Savior Jesus Christ, they are again entangled." Our homes are entangled in sin and distractions because we've made a choice to be entangled. Occasionally, we get on fire for God and God fills our homes, but soon we get lax and again we become entangled in sin and spiritual apathy. We spiritually bounce back and forth, and our families are torn apart because we have no consistency in our role as the Doorkeepers. That inconsistency comes from us not being on guard to watch at the door. That job belongs to the man of the house.

In order to be the spiritual Doorkeeper of your home, you must first have the Spirit of God! There must have been a time in your life when you accepted Jesus as your personal Lord and Savior. Many men walk through life trying to be a spiritual leader without having the Spirit of the living God in them. We had two deacons in our church that came to realize that they had never been saved. Years before, they went forward in our church and were baptized, but they had never asked Jesus to come into their hearts and forgive them of their sins. Have you ever been saved by the blood of Jesus? If not, you will never be the spiritual Doorkeeper of your home!

I believe God wants each of us to be certain of our salvation. I'd like to ask you to close your eyes and remember back in your childhood when your mother or grandmother was baking cookies in the kitchen. Your mind's eye is a powerful thing. You'll be able to clearly see the kitchen, the pots and pans, and the cabinet top. You'll smell the cookies or a cake cooking, anxiously awaiting the first bite. In the same way, your mind's eye can also go back to the time you accepted Christ as your Lord and Savior. Now close your eyes and remember back when you were saved by the blood of Jesus. I can remember back 52 years ago as clear as if it was yesterday. I was kneeling on an old floor full of knotholes beside an old bed. I read that familiar verse of scripture, John 3:16, that God so loved me that he gave His son, Jesus, and if I would believe in Him, I would not perish but have everlasting life. By reading Romans 3:23, I realized that I was a sinner. Then, as I read Romans 6:23, I began to understand that the wages of my sin deserved eternal death, but the gift of God is eternal life through Jesus Christ our Lord. In Romans 10:9, I read that if I would pray confessing with my mouth the Lord Jesus and believe in my heart that God had raised Him from the dead, I WOULD BE SAVED!! That day, I did just that. I received eternal life, and my life has never been the same again.

If you can't remember a time when you confessed your sins and accepted Jesus as your Lord and Savior, you'll never be able to become the spiritual Doorkeeper of your home. But it's not too late. Today is the day that God is giving you the opportunity to accept Him. You can bow your head right where you are and ask Him to come into your heart and life. If you do become saved, be sure and share your newfound faith with someone today.

In the chapters to come, you will learn the true job of a spiritual Doorkeeper. May God's precious Holy Spirit convict, instruct, and excite you about the peace that will come into your home as you fulfill the spiritual role God has given us.

"If you confess with your mouth Jesus as Lord, and believe in your heart that God raised Him from the dead, you shall be saved."

—Romans 10:9

PERSONAL SPIRITUAL INSIGHTS

1. Are you hearing the spiritual moaning and groaning going on in your family? Write down what you are seeing and hearing, no matter how small those sights and sounds may be!

2. Whose job is it to be the spiritual Doorkeeper of your home?

   Write down the things that might be getting in your way of you being the spiritual Doorkeeper.

3. In order to be a spiritual Doorkeeper, what must be within you?

4. Close your eyes and picture something pleasant in your childhood. Can you see it clearly with your mind's eye? Yes or No (circle one). Now, close your eyes again and go back to you salvation experience. Write in you own words the experience you see.

If you aren't certain that you've trusted in Christ to save you and forgive you, speak privately to a Christian friend, your pastor, or bow your head right where you are and ask Jesus to come into your life. I suggest you write down your prayer.

Share this good news of your salvation experience with someone right away! It will strengthen your commitment! Praise God!!!!!

My perspective...

Ronnie Gillum

As my wife and I look into the face of our newest grandson, we are once again reminded of God's grace and His perfect timing. Cole wasn't due for another four weeks, yet here is a strong healthy baby boy. He is a reminder of the most awesome blessing and responsibility God gives us.

Being raised in a Christian home, I'd always known about the love and power of God, but it was never as real to me as it has become in the last couple of years. After failed marriages, God laid out his plan and brought my wife and me together. We were determined that this marriage would be as God had meant marriage to be. We knew it would have to center around Him and His plans for this new blended family. My wife often tells people that God had to have brought us together because no man would voluntarily move into a house full of women! I had already been incredibly blessed as a single father to be able to raise my daughter during her teenage years. I now faced three new daughters, two of them teenagers still at home, with all the joys and craziness that goes with that.

We have learned that God puts people into your life for specific purposes. Just as I know that God brought Melanie and the girls into my life to join our families, Sonny and Delores Guess also came into our lives as leaders in our Sunday School department. Before the Doorkeeper Ministry even began, God had already given the message to Sonny that he is now sharing with every ear that will listen. As always, God's timing is perfect! Sonny began sharing with us the importance of the man being the head and guardian of the home, and the role of the father guarding and protecting those that God has put into his care.

While I had been active in Promise Keepers, hearing these words this time had a whole new meaning in my life. God began to change my heart. The things around me didn't change, but the way I reacted to them did. God gave me a heart that saw beyond the actions of people right down to the cause of that action. He gave me a heart slow to anger and quick to pray. I found myself praying for those that brought hurt or confusion to our family instead of casting blame. My wife and I have seen so many miraculous things happen as God changed our hearts and began to let us become a part of what He was doing.

As we fill our home with prayer, we are watching our girls grow and turn into women God is going to use in powerful ways. We have learned to speak the blessings of God on this family and expect the very best from Him. The more I pray, the more I feel God working in my life. The things that didn't seem to be very important suddenly became very clear to me. I had become very lonely during the last few years before Melanie and I met, and an eighteen pack of beer put me to bed every night. After we married, I still would have a couple to "unwind" when I got home. It didn't seem like a big deal to me—until it became a big deal to God. The closer my walk with God, the more it bothered me. At this point, I didn't want anything getting in the way of what He wanted to do in my life. I prayed that He would take that desire from me. The fact that I was able to just walk away from it was nothing short of God's power and mercy in full force in my life.

I know that God is going to use this ministry to wake the men of this country up and make them realize the value of what they hold in their homes. They say that a child's first impression of God is through their father, and I pray that this ministry will make that impression one of protection, guidance and unconditional love and mercy. God bless this ministry and Sonny and Delores for the boldness to speak the words God has given them with the love God has given them for the men of this country.

It's a Choice

When the Scripture says in Joshua 24:15, "Choose you this day whom you will serve," what kind of choice do I have? You see, when I became a born again Christian, God didn't take my free will away from me. I can choose to serve Him or choose not to serve Him. The choice is mine. In other words, as you are reading this right now, you have a choice—the choice about becoming the Doorkeeper of your home. As you look at your home and family right now, is your home a wreck? Is there turmoil within the walls of your house? If there is, I can assure you that God is not controlling your home, and it is your responsibility to see that it's brought back under God's leadership. Today, right now, you'll make a choice, either to be the spiritual leader, the Doorkeeper of your home, or you'll choose to keep your home in turmoil and go on through life allowing Satan to totally disrupt the relationships of your family. If that happens, joy will be nowhere in sight! Amazingly, most men would lay down their lives for their families if they were being *physically* attacked, but when that family is being spiritually attacked, that same man will sit quietly by and watch his home be torn apart by Satan and all the foes of hell.

What is your choice today?

Being the Doorkeeper of your home means that you put first things first, and the first thing you must do is love your wife. In Ephesians 5:25, Paul writes to husbands and tells us, "You must love [your wife] as Christ loved the church." I Peter 3:7 states, "If you do not love and give honor unto her, your prayers will not be answered." Loving your wife is far more than a physical encounter. Loving your wife is done with both words and actions. In Hebrews 10:24, the Scripture encourages us "to stimulate" her "to love and good works." What does that mean? It means that if you want to be king in your home, you have to treat her like a queen. Do special things for your wife that make her feel special: send flowers for no reason except that you love her, write her a note of appreciation and affection and put it under her pillow, help the kids do their homework or give them baths, get them ready for bed, or a multitude of other things you can think of to do. My wife and I do special things for each other. I never get up in the morning without drinking my first cup of coffee she has brought me in bed. She comes home from work an hour after I do, so I usually have supper on the table when she gets home—love and good works. Yes, we are like any other couple. We have our differences, but we have chosen to make the Lord the head of our home, and our marriage has lasted 42 years so far. Praise the Lord!

It's important to keep the communication channel open between you and your wife. Some of us find it difficult to express our feelings to our spouse. We hold our emotions in, but resentment builds up and explodes one day for no obvious, immediate reason. We need to learn to live with a constant flow of forgiveness. This means that I forgive her before she ever does anything to me. Then, on even her worst day, I can quickly forgive her so that resentment doesn't build up in me and sour our relationship. I've already chosen to swim in a sea of forgiveness, so I can quickly ask for forgiveness and quickly forgive. When we have problems with our wives, we must learn to do what Isaac did in Genesis 26:12-22. When the enemy came and filled up his well, he moved and dug another well. But his enemy kept pursuing him, so he moved and dug another well. He did it over and over again until he was finally left alone. We should do the same in our marriage. When we have a problem, forgive and forget. How often must we do this? Over and over again "until death do us part." We have a saying in our family that God gave us: "If it won't matter ten years from now, it really doesn't matter."

One of the greatest times you can have with your wife is to have a regular time to pray with her every day. At 6:45 a.m.

each morning, our family and friends know not to call us. This is a special time that Delores and I have set aside and commit only to prayer. We pray for each other, our children and their families, our Sunday school class members, our church family and staff, our community, our nation and national leaders. Our time together praying for our family is the most precious. We have three children and their spouses, and eight precious grandchildren. We pray for our children and their spouses to honor God in their work and all they do that day. We pray for all our grandchildren to come to know Jesus, and five of the eight have already trusted Him. What a blessing! This time of taking our family to the throne of God is one of the highlights of our day. Through prayer, we have seen God do great miracles in the relationships of our family. When we see things in our family going astray, we begin to pray. We only instruct when they ask us for input.

Prayer is one of our most powerful weapons in spiritual battle. You and your wife should set up a structured time right now to pray over your family. The power of God through prayer is mightier than thousands of words of instruction because you are allowing the most powerful force on this earth, the Holy Spirit, to do the convicting and correcting. Trust me. We have watched miracles in relationships happen before our very eyes through prayer.

I also think one of the most important things a man can do is to love his wife in front of his children. Delores and I kiss and hug each other in front of our kids. This sets an example of the true love that God has for a man and his wife. After all, He created a man and woman to have this type of love relationship. As your children look on, they witness what a healthy marriage relationship should look like, and they'll seek that relationship for themselves when the time comes to find God's mate for them. One day I was kissing and hugging my wife in the kitchen, and my oldest son came into the room. He was only 2 years old. I looked down to discover that he had no clothes on. Before I could say anything, he said, "Mommy when you get through loving daddy, would you get me some toilet paper?" We thought it was funny at the time, but I soon realized that he had recognized that hugging mommy was important! To this day, all my children are very loving and affectionate with their spouses. This heritage will be passed down for generations as our offspring observe their parents in a loving relationship.

Of course, you'll experience times when you and your spouse have differences of opinion. Let me encourage you not to display anger and hurting words toward each other in front of your children. Your bedroom serves as a great place to get these differences straightened out. In these discussions, remember that God made you both equal—He just gave you different roles. For years, I'm afraid that I never let my wife have her say! I was the head of the home, and I made all the decisions! What a huge mistake!! I missed out on years of awesome wisdom and love that she could have contributed to our decisions, and with her input, I would have made better decisions along the way. By the way, your bedroom is also a great place to say, "I'm sorry" and make up! That's convenient because you are already there! Once you have made things right with each other, the joy of the Lord will be returned in your relationship and family.

Praise God for our brides!

"Husbands, love your wives, just as Christ also loved the church and gave Himself up for her."

—Ephesians 5:25

PERSONAL SPIRITUAL INSIGHTS

1. Survey your home in your mind right now. Describe the level of turmoil or peace within the walls of your home. Write down several reasons for your answer.

2. Based on the information in this chapter, how do you measure up when it comes to loving your wife? Write down five or six things you do (or that you could do) to show your love to her.

3. Are there unresolved differences between you and your wife? If so, make a list of those things that are driving you apart.

4. Can you imitate Isaac and ask for forgiveness and dig another well? What would this conversation look like? Write down exactly what you plan to say to her—with no excuses and without blaming her in the least.

5. Do you show affection to your wife in the presence of your children? Yes or No (circle one). (Remember the best thing you can do for your children is to show them that you love their mother.) How would your children describe the affection between you and your wife?

6. Do you pray daily with your wife? Yes or No (circle one). Write down in your own words a commitment to find a time to pray with her. How would a consistent time of prayer with her affect your relationship with her, with your children, and with God?

My perspective...

Melanie Gillum

I don't know that we can ever put into words what this ministry has meant to Ronnie and me. The way it has changed our lives . . . and the things Ronnie has learned that filter down into my life and the lives of our daughters and son-in-laws . . . the feeling that a wife gets when her husband says, "God put you on my heart today, and I pulled the truck over and prayed for you" . . . when that same man prays for people that mistreat him or for the father of his stepchildren to have a closer relationship with them . . . that's God! That's God moving in a man's life and changing everyone around him by the example he sets.

Through your teaching and God's Word, our home has become a real dwelling place for God. It's a true refuge from the world we live in. It doesn't mean we don't have problems like everyone else, but it means we never face them alone, and we face them with a peace in the middle of the storm! I've always loved the line in the song that says sometimes in the middle of that storm, "He doesn't calm the storm, He calms His child."

Because of this ministry, we truly are believing and living the conviction: "As for me and my house, we will serve the Lord." We love you and Delores, and we have cherished your prayers during our storms! May God's blessings abound in this ministry and your lives!

Bless Your Children

One of the most life-changing things you can do for your children is to bless them. In order to bless them, first of all we need to realize that children are made to God's specifications, and all of them are created special and unique. God, in His great wisdom, sees to it that no two people are made alike, so we need to find different ways to bless each child. Some children love sports, and some love books. It's important to remember that they are made in the image of God, not in your image. Don't try to make your children into something that you want them to be. Instead, encourage them to be the person God designed them to be. Remember, things that we see as our child's biggest weaknesses, God may see as their greatest strengths.

While raising your children, remember that in I Peter 5:3-6, we are told to be "clothed in humility." Now, humility is not something we have when we are born. Most of us learn to be humble through painful circumstances in life that teach us this wonderful trait. We are born with a lot of pride in our hearts. When our first-born son was placed in my grandfather's hands, he held the baby up and told my wife and me that he was just a little sinner. My wife had a fit! I said, "Papa, I think you said the wrong thing!" and he replied, "No I didn't. You wait a few weeks and you will see." Papa was right! The Bible says that we are "all born in sin."

It's certainly difficult to be humble when you are trying to raise a rebellious child. One day as I left the house for work, I asked my son to mow the yard. I came home at lunch to find that he had not obeyed me. I struggled with anger in those years, and at this defying act, I was more than displeased. I threw open the door to find him lying in the floor watching television. I began to sharply explain my dissatisfaction that the yard had not been mowed as I had ordered. He told me the lawnmower wouldn't start, and that was the reason he couldn't mow the yard. I dragged him outside to watch me start the mower so he could do the task I had commanded him to do. I cranked, I cranked, and I cranked while he watched patiently. Finally, he said, "I told you it wouldn't start." This only added fuel to my fire. I asked him to go into the house while I angrily worked on the mower. I put a new spark plug into the mower, and it started right away. I stuck my head in the door to announce to him that he better have the yard mowed before I got home that afternoon!

After returning to my office, the convicting power of the Holy Spirit revealed to me that I 'd wrongly accused my son of something he hadn't done. All afternoon I was saddened that I'd hurt my child by the angry words I 'd spoken to him. When I returned home that afternoon, the yard was neatly mowed as I 'd asked. I called him into our bedroom to speak with him. His first words were, "Daddy, I mowed the yard. What did I do wrong?" As tears rolled down my cheeks, I put my hand on his shoulder and asked him to forgive me for falsely accusing him when it was not his fault. He looked at me and said, "Daddy, that's okay. I forgive you."

How many times have you wrongly accused your children and failed to go back to them and asked for forgiveness? Be clothed in humility. It'll make a huge difference in your family!

Bless your children with words. By the words that we choose, we have a choice to bless them or curse them. It's beautiful to watch as my nephew, Greg, and his wife, Sally Sue, bless their children with words. The other day I observed Greg with his oldest daughter, loving and playing with her. He was telling her how beautiful she was and what a special little girl God had given them. I was taken back to memories of my childhood. Our families back then weren't taught how to bless their children. I was born with a birthmark on my forehead. The kids often teased me about the birthmark, and I fought them. I received hundreds of spankings at school and home for fighting. Then it happened!!! I went into the 5th grade in our little country school. We had a new teacher, and she was going over the list of students. When she called my name and she saw me, she walked over to me and told me that my birthmark was beautiful. Before that day, no one had ever told me that. She told me that God had made me special. What a difference her words made in my life. My conduct grades went from straight F's to straight A's. God had made me special. What an awesome thought!! Several years ago they came up with laser surgery that could remove the birthmark. My parents called and said they would pay to have it removed. I instantly replied, "Why? God gets the glory from my birthmark." Sometimes I'm in a store waiting to check out and a small child in front of me will say, "Man, what is that on your head?"

I just say, "Oh, I'm just getting bald."

They say," No, that red place on your head."

By this time, their mother is embarrassed to tears and apologizing to me. I explain that it is O.K because God made me special. As I look at the child, I share that God made him or her special too. I ask for their little thumb and share with them that their thumbprint is the only one like it in the entire world. God really made you special, and He really loves you! Bless your children with words!!!

Ephesians 3:17-19 states, "We must root and ground our children in the love of God." It's the Doorkeeper's responsibility to instill the Word of God in his children. Let me reemphasize: This shouldn't be left solely up to the wife. When an oak tree is planted, there's a deep hole dug in the ground in which to plant the tree. As the roots of the tree begin to grow deep in the soil, the solid foundation gives the tree stability. One day the wind will blow with a mighty force, but the tree will be able to withstand the pressure because it has been rooted and grounded. The same must be true for our children. A child who has been taught the Word of God and memorized hundreds of its precious verses will be able to stand during the storms that life brings.

One day your children will be 18 years of age—they'll know it's time to leave home, and so will you. You have only been given stewardship of them, and then it will be time to turn them out into the world to fend for themselves. Trust me, those who have been rooted and grounded in the Word of God will be able to stand during the tough times. They will make godly decisions and serve the King of Kings and Lord of Lords, Jesus Christ!!!

Fun and laughter should fill our homes. Sometimes I think I took life too seriously when my children were young. I spent very little time listening to my children and their needs. The sad thing is I can't go back and change anything. What's done is done. I pray that you will listen in this area to a dad who messed up. Spend more time listening to your children. Ask for their input more often, and whatever you do, don't take life too seriously. Sometimes we push our kids to make a straight "A" report card, but it's more for us than for the child. Some parents want the community and the world to know that their little Johnny or little Suzy is so smart, but sometimes I don't think God is in that at all. The parents are pushing the kids to excel for bragging rights, not for the benefit of the child. It's okay to expect your children to do the best they can in school, but they must still be allowed to have a normal childhood. Some children feel that all they ever do is have their nose in a book, and they miss out on the fun and laughter of childhood.

I learned that I had but one shot to raise my babies. I did some things really well, but I did some things very wrong. I know one thing: I was not only raising children. I was also making memories that would last a lifetime. Sometimes Delores and I go back in time and remember those precious memories. We relive and celebrate the fun and laughter we enjoyed during those times. Soak in the sunshine of the great times raising your children because you are making precious memories.

"Christ may dwell in your hearts through faith, and that you being rooted and grounded in love, may be able to comprehend with all the saints what is breadth and length and height and depth, and to know the love of Christ which surpasses knowledge, that you may be filled up to all the fullness of God."

—Ephesians 3:17–19

PERSONAL SPIRITUAL INSIGHTS

1. What would it mean to your children if you encourage them to be all that God wants them to be instead of forcing them to be what you want them to be?

2. In I Peter 5:3-6, the Bible says we are to be clothed in _____. What would (or does) that look like in your relationships with your wife and your children?

3. Write down several incidences in which you were not humble, and as a result, you hurt your wife.

Your children:

Have you asked for forgiveness in each of these situations? It's never too late. I suggest going to each one today so that these hurts may be resolved, forgiven, and forgotten! What great cleansing you'll experience in your relationships!

4. In blessing your children, write down some of the words you could use.

5. List ways in which you can root and ground your children in the love of God!

6. Is it fun for your wife and children to live in your home? Yes or No (circle one)

   List your children's names below. Beside each name list their personality traits, gifts, and talents. What are some ways you can affirm these characteristics in them and build their confidence?

7. Write a plan for developing each child into the person God designed him or her to be.

My perspective...

A letter to my husband from Sally Sue Harriss

My dearest Greg,

There are so many qualities about you that I love. When I think of the role you play as my husband, I'm overwhelmed with gratefulness. You are my gentle giant. You protect our family and provide for us so well. You have always prayed me through the hard times and given me perspective when I haven't been able to see the wonder of our Creator.

I love that you always give credit for everything in our lives to our Almighty Father. It's truly a blessing to be married to you and to share my life with a man whom I believe with all my heart is the most amazing husband and father that I know—you bring so much joy and laughter to our home. You aren't afraid to laugh and have fun with the kids, and as a result, our home is filled with joy. You have assumed the role of being an intercessor in prayer for our children. You effectively pray for our family, and for that, I'm thankful.

Thank you for all you do. I know that because of your faith and example, our children will grow up knowing that their father is a man of his word and that their dad prays for them. If I could only say one word to you, I would say "THANKS!"

I love you, and I'm so proud to be your wife and the mother of our children. I thank God for you!!

Arrows in the Hand
of a Mighty Man

I guess there have been hundreds (if not thousands) of books written on how to discipline a child. Everything from "time out" to spanking to whispering in their ears that whatever they were doing isn't very nice. We all have our opinions about disciplining our children, but the Word of God is very direct when it comes to this subject. The book of Proverbs is full of pointed instructions concerning the use of the rod to discipline a child. In America, we have chosen to get away from this form of discipline, but we have paid dearly for this decision. We have raised generations who have not been disciplined, and our children—and our nation—have paid the price. Our schools have removed the rod of discipline due to liberal court decisions, and the results are showing in the number of prisons we have to build to hold adults who were raised without the hand of discipline.

My question is this: If children never learn to respect and obey their parents, how will they ever learn to respect and obey God? I believe that there's a correct way to use the rod, and it's not always necessary to use this form of discipline. The Bible says that if I love my son, I will discipline him. Whatever form of discipline you choose must be used in love and not in anger! This is a tough area for a lot of us Doorkeepers. We need God's wisdom, but the rewards are awesome as we train up our children to have obedience and respect toward all people in authority, especially God!

By now, I'm sure you understand that I not only believe in using the rod when needed, but I believe God's word expects us, as the Doorkeepers, to handle most of the discipline. One day I came home from a business trip, and my wife met me at the door. There wasn't a kiss or a hug awaiting me, but an index finger motioning for me to come into our bedroom. It seems my son who was 16 and weighed 250 pounds had disobeyed his mother. She explained to me that she tried to spank him, and he held her hands by her side and said; "Now momma, you don't want to do that!"

Well, to say the least, my bride was hot! I asked, "Why in the world did you try to spank him? Why didn't you wait until I got home?" By this time I was lying on the bed rolling with laughter. I can assure you, that reaction to her plight was not a good thing!

Soon, I regained my composure and went into his bedroom to confront him. I asked him why he refused to let his mother spank him. He responded that she couldn't hurt him, so there was no reason to do it. I asked, "Son, if your coach told you to bend over and take a lick, what would you do?"

He said, "I'd bend over and take a lick."

I then asked, "If your principal told you to bend over and take a lick, what would you do?"

He said, "I'd bend over and take a lick."

I told him, "When the mother who brought you into this world, who loves you more than anyone else, who takes care of you when you're sick, washes your clothes, and feeds you real good says, 'Bend over and take a lick,' what should you do?"

He said, "Bend over and take a lick."

I said, "I think you better bend over because I am going to give you a lick—and by the way, I assure you it'll hurt!"

Men, I want you to know that the Doorkeeper is responsible to God for the discipline that's used in his home.

I began to study Psalm 127:3-5, and God gave me a wonderful truth about children being arrows in the hands of a mighty man. As your children grow up, they represent your name. I explained to my sons, "You've been given a name that you'll carry the rest of your lives. That name is Guess. My grandfather was a man of integrity, and my father was a man of integrity. Lord willing, I've been a man of integrity, and you represent my name everywhere you go." Where will that integrity come from in our children? It will come from the way we raise them!

I'm a bow hunter, and as I read this passage of Scripture, I thought a lot about the structure of an arrow. A few years ago, I was privileged to take a 5x5 bull elk with my bow in Colorado. I understand one thing about going bow hunting: You practice, practice and practice to become proficient with your bow. As I looked at the arrows, the Lord gave me an analogy that certainly gives this Scripture a lot of meaning to me. The arrow is made up of basically three parts: the broad head, the shaft, and the vanes. The *broad head* speaks of the Word of God. In Hebrews 4:12 the writer states, "The Word of God is quick, powerful, and sharper than a two-edged sword." The *shaft* speaks of the moral and spiritual raising of a child. The shaft must be perfectly straight if the arrow is to fly right. The *vanes*, the feathers on the back end of an arrow, usually come in three. They speak of God the Father, Son, and Holy Spirit. You see, the vanes are the guidance system of that arrow, and it won't fly straight without them. So, as Doorkeepers, we must spend a lot of time instilling the Word of God into our children, training them to have spiritual values and good morals so that when they are released into the world from our bow (our home), they'll be guided by the Father, Son, and Holy Spirit.

My prayer is that we'll raise more godly arrows to fly out into the world and share the love of Jesus, become great citizens in all walks of life, including Christian judges, Christian representatives and senators, and yes, even the President of the United States.

Those arrows are in your quiver right now. Will you as the Doorkeeper do your part for the Lord to make a difference in the world with the children you are raising?

"Behold, children are a gift of the Lord; The fruit of the womb is a reward. Like arrows in the hand of a warrior, so are the children of one's youth. How blessed is the man whose quiver is full of them; They shall not be ashamed, when they speak with their enemies in the gate."

—Psalm 127:3-5

PERSONAL SPIRITUAL INSIGHTS

1. In your opinion, is disciplining your children important? Yes or No (circle one). Read Proverbs 13:24, 19:18, 22:15, 23:13, 22:6. After reading these scriptures, write down what these verses are saying to you as the Doorkeeper.

2. What are some of the different forms of discipline?

3. Consider the personalities of each of your children. Which

form of discipline would be best administered to each of your children? Explain your choices.

4. Describe the importance of keeping a good name.

5. Since your children are arrows in your quiver, list each child again. Beside their names, list the weak areas that you see in each child. How might God view these as strengths? What can you do to help them in each area (consider the broad head, shaft, and vanes)?

6. Are you willing to work to see that the arrows in which God has entrusted you will fly straight when they leave your bow? Yes or No (circle one) What can you do to ensure that your arrows will fly straight?

My perspective...

Chris Kethan

As the father of 4 beautiful girls and the husband of the most beautiful woman in the world, I can hardly express my overwhelming gratitude to Sonny for his Doorkeeper Ministries. The words and direction Sonny gives are long overdue and need to be heard by every man who has a family to bring safely through this world.

Whenever I find myself feeling unprepared in the battle against Satan and his constant attacks on my family, I turn to principles Sonny has taught me. The Doorkeeper Ministries is the "playbook" that millions of fathers and I can use in our daily lives.

I pray that Sonny's ministry will touch many men to break the cycle of broken homes, fatherless children, and divorces plaguing our nation. Thank you, Sonny, from the bottom of my heart for being the voice that gave me a new outlook and instruction for my role as the Doorkeeper of my home. God bless you.

Take a Stand!

In Ephesians 6:13-14, Paul says, "Wherefore take unto you the whole armor of God that ye may be able to withstand in the evil day, and having done all to stand, stand!" As the Doorkeeper for my family, that means I put one foot at one side of the door of my home and one foot at the other side of the door. My role is to defend the people God has entrusted to me. As verse 14 continues, Paul encourages the Christian how to put on the whole armor of God. You see, as the Doorkeeper of my home, I'm to stand at the door of my home, having my "feet shod with the preparation of the gospel of peace." I "gird my loins with the truth" of Jesus Christ, and I "put on the breastplate of righteousness." I carry "the sword of the Spirit" of the Lord and "the shield of faith," and I "put on the helmet of salvation." I'm now totally protected against Satan and his army from penetrating my home. I do this each and every day—then and only then am I the Doorkeeper of my home. There will be nothing coming in my home or going out of my home that my eye won't catch. I've put up a godly roadblock at the door of my home to protect my wife and children from Satan and the deceptions and attacks of this world.

As the Doorkeeper for your home, this is your biblical responsibility as the man of your house! Don't waiver. Stand on godly principles. Don't just trust your instincts, because Satan can influence your instincts! Look in the Bible, and stand on the Word of God as your guide!

Declare God as the head of your home! When you do this, you may have to clean out your home to get rid of anything that displeases Him. There may be magazines, books, music, clothes, and pictures that you will have to throw out—not put in a drawer until you don't feel as strongly about the Lord's purposes, but thrown in the trash and hauled off to the dump. You will need to monitor the television, the radio, and other forms of media, both audio and visual. One day I came into my home and found my son and some football friends lying in the floor watching a movie. As I listened from the other room, I heard a word I didn't like. I walked in and saw a scene in the movie that I did not approve of, so I walked over to the television and hit the eject button on the VCR. The guys instantly reacted, "What are you doing?" I announced that I had chosen for my home to be a house of God, and this type of movie was inappropriate. One of the boys said they could watch it at his house. I said that that would be fine, but when they needed a place to come away from the garbage of the world, they were welcome to come to our home. As for me and my house, we're going to honor God! We lived on one of the main streets in town. Many of the classmates of my children often stopped by and had meals with our family. Some of them later told us that their feet were under our table more than their own. We fed them, loved them, but most of all, we got to share Jesus with them. Some of them came to know the Lord. Praise be to God!

One day a man told me that his home was a wreck. There was always arguing, shouting, confusion, and total dissention the minute he walked in the door. I asked him questions about his family and what they were doing. He began to cry and explained that his son usually came home, went straight to his room, locked the door, and refused to allow his dad to come into the room.

I asked, "Do you have a screwdriver in your toolbox?" "Yeah, I have several." he responded. "What for?"

I explained, "You can unscrew the hinges so you can take his door off. Get prayed up, get into his room, and you'll find the reason for the unrest in your home!" I advised him to take everything that was ungodly out of there, build a fire in the back yard, and burn it all up. Then peace would return to his home! Well, he did just that. When he entered his son's room, there were sadistic pictures on the walls, shirts that promoted Satan hanging in the closet, CDs that glorified killing, and other garbage that I am not free to share in this book. He gathered them up, built a fire in his back yard, and burned them up. He explained that while he was carrying them out, the hair was standing up on his arms. You see, Satan had permeated his home a little at a time until he had infested the whole house. It's the Doorkeeper's job to clean out the ungodly things that enter his home and stand at the door to see that they never return again.

Beware! Satan will try to creep into your home in subtle ways to disrupt your family. In I Peter 5:8, Peter says that Satan "is like a roaring lion seeking whom he may devour." We can usually recognize an abrupt attack of Satan, but after we make the commitment to be the Doorkeeper of our homes, he will try to get into our homes totally unnoticed! He will try to distract you and get your mind off your job as the Doorkeeper. One year on opening day of gun season, I went to my deer stand before daylight and opened the door of the stand. There he was, a little mouse looking me in the eye saying, "Good morning." I don't know who was startled the most! He ran down the square tubing of my ladder. I thought, *Well, he's gone. He won't bother me any more.* I got into my stand and began to hunt. A little later, I looked down at the door of my stand, and I could see the little mouse's nose sticking through the crack in the door. I took my hat and swatted at him. He was definitely a distraction.

I had to laugh as I thought of a little boy who came home one day and asked his dad, "How much water does a mouse have in him?" The father replied that he had no idea, but they could look it up on the Internet and possibly find the answer. The dad asked his son, "Why did you ask such a question?"

His son replied, "Well, today, a little mouse ran across the classroom floor at school and ran up the teacher's leg. She grabbed him and squeezed a quart of water out of him!" This is of course a funny story, but it's a fact that even when Satan uses small things to get into our homes, the results can be disastrous. The Doorkeeper's job is to sharpen his spiritual skills in order to spot even the smallest move of Satan.

Last but not least, display Scripture in every room of your home. During the Passover, the children of Israel experienced the last plague God inflicted on Egypt. They were instructed to get a spotless lamb, slay it, and put its blood on the doorpost and lintel of their door. Then they were to take the lamb in the house, roast it and eat it all. God said, "When I see the blood, I will pass over you!" The power of the death angel was broken that night in their homes because the lamb's blood was posted on the door! I also believe that the power of Satan will be broken in my home when I post the Word of God at my front door and in every room of my home. You can walk through my house and find scripture in every room. I don't care if you are on the commode in my home, you will be able to read the Word of the living God!

Having the peace of God in your home gives your family a place of rest and comfort to enjoy after battling the world all day at work or school. The greatest way to have a peaceful home and keep Satan out is to play spiritual music in your home 24 hours a day. The Bible says, "God inhabits the praises of His people." He lives in the praises of His people, and Christian music offers wonderful praise to God. Understand this: Where God is, Satan will not come. When we play spiritual praises to God in our home 24 hours a day, God promises to be there and Satan will not be there! Praise the Lord! What a truth! In our home, we play spiritual music in our bedroom, our living room, kitchen, and even in the garage! One day my daughter-in-law came and said, "Pops, your home is so peaceful. I just want to lay on the floor in the family room and absorb the peace." Your home can be like this, too. May God bless you as you put these practical suggestions to work in your home. Then you can truly proclaim, "Jesus is Lord, and Satan, you're toast!"

"Therefore, take up the full armor of God, that you may be able to resist in the evil day, and having done everything, to stand firm, stand firm therefore, having girded your loins with truth, and having put on the breastplate of righteousness, and having shod your feet with the preparation of the gospel of peace; in addition to all, taking up the shield of faith with which you will be able to extinguish all the flaming missiles of the evil one, and take the helmet of salvation, and the sword of the Spirit, which is the word of God."

—Ephesians 6:13-17

PERSONAL SPIRITUAL INSIGHTS

1. After reading this chapter, explain in you own words what it means to protect your home as the spiritual Doorkeeper.

2. Are you willing to declare God as the head of your home? List, as the Holy Spirit brings to your mind, things that must be cleaned out of your home. Be sensitive to the Holy Spirit's conviction. Don't resist Him. And remember, some of the things you need to clean out may be yours!

The last thought you had and did not write down is creating a major wall that will keep God's holiness from your home! WRITE IT DOWN!

3. Like the man who had the wayward son and cleaned out his son's room, do you have the spiritual strength to remove the above list of things from your home? Yes of No (circle one).

   If your answer is "yes," you're truly becoming the spiritual Doorkeeper God intends for you to be!

   If not, you are failing God, your wife, and your children! Pray until God gives you the strength to accomplish this task.

4. List some ways that Satan can creep into your house and slip by unnoticed.

5. Look back at some of the things we've done in our home, and list some powerful but easy ways that you can keep Satan out of your home.

What are some habits and practices that can bring the peace of God into your home permanently?

Then do it! Remember, your home must be cleaned out first!!!

My perspective...

A Pensive Wife

The Doorkeeper message was awesome! As I listened, I began to think of how we need more men to be the Doorkeepers of their homes.

I love my husband and have had 50 wonderful years of marriage, but now I see more than ever that he failed to be the spiritual doorkeeper of our home. Consequently, only one child out of four is concerned about spiritual things. Although they were taken to church and had the Bible read to them when they were young, the strong stand was not there by the Doorkeeper. I continue to pray that someday they will come back before it's too late.

I know that God will use this message because I'm convinced it's what Christian men desperately need to hear today!

Flood Your Mind with the Word of God

As the Doorkeeper of your home, flood your mind with the Word of God. I regularly read the news and watch television updates about our Commander-in-Chief, the President of the United States. I've never had the privilege of meeting him and visiting with him, but I respect and pray for him daily. We are in a war with terrorist around the world, and our President makes decisions every day to protect our freedoms and affect our families for generations to come. Sometimes we are glued to the television as we watch the tragedy of bloodshed and heartache unfolding before our very eyes. Our soldiers have a difficult task, but they would be confused and ineffective in battle if they didn't receive instructions from the commander-in-chief. In the same way, there is a spiritual war going on right now in your community. The difference for the Doorkeeper is that he has a chance not only to visit daily with our spiritual Commander-in-Chief, but we can receive instructions from the Word of God and the Holy Spirit that indwells us.

My question to you is: Do you connect with God every day by reading the Word of God and allowing the Holy Spirit to teach you how to have wisdom to perform the duties of the Doorkeeper of your home for that particular day? Reading God's Word will strengthen and empower you! Through the truth of Scripture, you'll have wisdom beyond your years, boldness to exert your spiritual authority as a Doorkeeper, and love for people in every situation you encounter. The effects of the godly decisions you make for your family will affect generations to come.

Set aside a time to have a family devotion with your family. It doesn't have to be long, but it will be a spiritual encouragement for the day for the whole family. Also, have a prayer time together to allow the Holy Spirit to soak the hearts of your family with the truths you learn that day. If you don't know how to lead a daily devotion, let me recommend an excellent one written just for you. The devotional is called *Our Daily Bread.* If you don't have one, you can find information on their web site. At our house, we read this devotional at our breakfast table every morning before we leave the house. You'll be stirred by the stories and truths from God's Word in this devotional. As the Doorkeeper and spiritual leader of your home, you should show your family that a time set aside to hear from our spiritual Commander-in-Chief is of utmost importance.

There are many great books to help you grow spiritually and lead your family. Some of these books are on CDs, which you can play in you vehicle as you go to work or travel on trips. Not long ago, I was driving to my deer lease, which is about a seven-hour drive from my home. My brother-in-law had given me a series of CDs on how to raise a boy to spiritual manhood. I thought, *Man, there are 18 CDs in this case. I'll never listen to all of these.* I left home with six of them in my truck stereo. When I'd listened to the last one, I pulled off the road and put in six more. By the time I got home, I had listened to all 18 and was gloriously blessed. God's Spirit has led men and women to write great spiritual material for you and me to be blessed so we can grow strong in our Lord.

"Thy word is a lamp to my feet and a light to my path."

—Psalm 119:105

PERSONAL SPIRITUAL INSIGHTS

1. Think about the past week. How often have you contacted the spiritual Commander-in-Chief? _____

   You can speak to Him in prayer. List the ways He can speak to you.

2. What are some of the benefits of leading a family devotion in your home?

3. Describe some practices and resources you can use to have meaningful devotional times with your family.

If you left this blank, it means that you have not planned time for one. Having a family devotion is your opportunity as the spiritual Doorkeeper to give spiritual leadership to your family. You might use the recommendation in this chapter to order *Our Daily Bread* or another resource that appeals to you. Don't neglect this effort! It's a very important part of your job.

4. List other avenues that are available for a man to be strengthened as a Doorkeeper.

My perspective...

Trish Guess

Thank you for your mission to teach the men of today to be the godly leaders of their homes that God intended them to be. God has blessed me and my two boys with the best gift a woman could ask for... a godly man.

Your mission was founded on the Biblical principles for being a godly man. These principles can be found in Ephesians 5:22 – 6:4. These verses outline the role of a godly man, husband and father.

Michael is an awesome husband. He loves me dearly, and I see it daily. He demonstrates his love for us through his eyes, hands and feet.

When I gaze into his eyes, I see love that is true, pure, and unconditional. I see his faithfulness and adoration for me. As the song goes, he "has his Father's eyes" (his Heavenly Father's). May God continue the vision for a godly world through Michael's eyes.

By watching Michael's hands, I see the touch of the Father. Michael uses his hands to provide income to meet the needs of our family. He takes the role of bread winner seriously. He tithes and gives as directed in the Bible. I see his hands as they hold and tickle our children in times of hurt and play. I feel gentle and caressing hands as he is a loving husband. Finally, I see hands that come together in prayer as he leads us daily to pray. May God continue to use Michael's hands in such a way as to please Him.

Michael's *feet* take him down the path of godliness. His feet don't trod where they shouldn't. They don't go to questionable places. They do, however, lead his family to church. They carry him to work and home where he leads by example. He walks with the Lord on a daily basis. I pray for God's continued blessings on my husband's feet.

Michael's service is an evidence of his godly walk. He serves as the Sunday school teacher for high school juniors and sings in the choir. I'm glad that he shows our family that it's important to serve others. He witnesses to anyone that God places on his heart, and he is selfless in his mission to win others for Christ. He is a role model for others who watch him.

I'm overwhelmed as a wife as I sit back and see all the ways God uses Michael to be the leader of our home and family. I think of the legacy he is leaving for our boys. As Caleb and Zachary grow, they are watching their dad and learning how to be godly men. They are learning how to care for and treat their own wives and families someday. God is preparing my boys to be the Doorkeepers of their homes by Michael's example.

Michael isn't perfect, but he's willing to admit and apologize when things aren't as they should be. He's my Prince Charming. (As the heir to the King of Kings and Lord of Lords, that makes him a prince.) He invites me to discuss important matters with him, and we make decisions together. I accept the final decisions that he makes and know that God has given him authority over me and my family—not for overpowering me or to be domineering, but to give wise counsel and use the wisdom God gave him to make smart decisions. I feel grateful that he takes charge. I know he will be the one answering to God for the decisions that come from our home. That, in itself, is a huge responsibility.

I'm praying for your ministry as you reach and teach many men across America, (and beyond) to become the godly Doorkeepers of their homes. God has given me and my boys a godly Doorkeeper, and we are truly blessed for it. I pray that as these men put their hearts, trust and homes in God's hands, and that God will put these gentlemen at the head of their homes where He intended for them to be.

God bless you all and your ministry!

Don't Accept the Unacceptable

Many Christians have been sold down the river, so to speak, when it comes to really believing that God is a living God who answers prayer! We pray, but our prayers lack the power of faith. Our minds have been absorbed by a philosophy called "Humanism," and this philosophy has deceived us about the existence, goodness, and greatness of Almighty God. We no longer live by faith, trusting God in our business and in our community, much less in our homes. We sit around and whimper when we see our children going the way of the world. Society excuses evil behavior by saying, "Everyone's doing it, and there is nothing you can do to change it." Too often, we just shrug our shoulders and mumble, "I guess I'll just have to accept it and go on." Then we sit idly by and watch our kids jump to every temptation to be accepted. We don't step in and offer God's truth and God's correction because we don't want to cause friction or disruption in our family.

In those times, the crying question is: Where is the Doorkeeper who has trained for the spiritual warfare? It's our responsibility to God to pull out the sword of the Spirit and be ready for the battle. We have prayed. The Word of God says that what we are praying about is His will, so we can stand straight and tall and announce to our children and the world that we won't accept the unacceptable! By the power of the Holy Spirit, the victory will be won. Remember the verse that says, "Greater is He that is within you than he that is in the world." This means that when we are going into battle with Satan and we know we are doing God's will, we will win EVERY time! Let me give you an example of this awesome concept God gave me.

My wife and I prayed for our children's salvation and their mates ever since they were in her womb. At a young age, they all gave their heart and life to Jesus Christ! Praise the Lord! We've also prayed for Christian spouses for them as well. On Thanksgiving weekend, my son, who was then 21, announced that he was bringing a young lady home with him for Thanksgiving. He was working about 300 miles from where we lived, and he had met her down there. When she walked into our home, I quietly asked myself, *Where in the world did he get her?* At the dinner table, we bowed our heads to give thanks for the food, and you could tell this young lady had never seen anyone do this before. The Holy Spirit quickly revealed to me that she wasn't a Christian. A couple of days later, it was time for them to leave, and my son invited me into the back yard to ask me what I thought about this lady he was going to marry. I quickly explained to him that she wasn't a Christian, and he wouldn't be marrying her unless she came to know Jesus. That's what I mean by taking a stand. She wasn't what we had prayed for, and it certainly wasn't God's will because His Word says, "Be ye not unequally yoked with unbelievers." I prayed in earnest as he left in rage. In no uncertain terms, he explained that he was 21, and I didn't have the right to tell him who he could marry. It was a six-hour drive home for him and this lovely lady, and as is our custom, he called me when he got home. As I listened to his voice, he was crying. He explained that she had told him that he had a strange family, and she didn't want to see him anymore. I tried not to show too much joy. God not only answered my prayer, but He had showed me that I didn't have to accept the unacceptable—including an unsaved spouse for my child.

Well, at that point, momma and I began to pray in earnest for a Christian spouse for my son. About nine months later, he called me. I could hear the excitement in his voice. He said, "Dad I think I've found her."

I said, "Okay son, tell me about her."

He said, "I was in the shoe store to get a pair of work boots, and a girl waited on me. She looked up at me and asked me if those shoes fit. She was so beautiful that it took me a little time to speak. As we were talking, I asked her out. She asked me if I was a Christian because she didn't go out with guys who weren't Christians.'"

I was elated! Today, these two have been married 16 years and have given Delores and me three beautiful granddaughters. You see, God proved that He was God and that He was waiting for the Doorkeeper to step in by faith and not accept the unacceptable!

You would think that one experience like this was enough for our family, but God wanted to test our faith again. This time it was through our daughter. Again, she was in her early 20's and dating a boy who wasn't a Christian. Much to my dismay, they were finally engaged, but I said, "No, I'm going to hold on to the fact that we've prayed, and God will honor our prayers."

As the wedding date drew closer, she asked if I was going to perform the ceremony. I told her, "No, I won't join you in an unequal yoke!"

Then a few days later, she asked me if I was going to wear a tuxedo when I walked her down the aisle. I replied, "I won't walk you down the aisle to marry an unsaved person!"

She asked me how much money she could spend. I replied, "Everything I have belongs to the Lord. I'm just a steward of what I have. Therefore, you can spend as much as you want, but mom and I won't be supplying any money because I'm responsible to God for how I use His funds."

It was two weeks before the wedding date, and the wedding was still on. Delores was having rigors, but I assured her that God was going to do His part. All we could do at this point was to pray. Guess what! God is the same yesterday, today, and forever! Glory to God—He did it again! A few days later, I noticed my daughter's little car coming down the driveway with the trunk wide open. She came in the house crying and said, "Daddy, it's off."

Again, I tried not to show too much joy. I asked her what had happened. She said, "He told me he wanted everything he had ever given me. I gave him back his ring. Then I told him I wanted everything I had given him. Daddy, I told him I wanted back that shirt he had on, those tennis shoes, and by the way, I think I gave him those Levis he was wearing. I stripped him down to his underwear in his front yard. I collected deer stands, deer feeders, and other hunting gear. I put them in my trunk and brought them to the house."

I was praising God for His faithfulness! Oh by the way, Christmas came early for me. She gave me all those goodies! WOW, what an awesome God we serve! Later, she met the man God had prepared for her. He was a football player and was saved through the Fellowship of Christian Athletes. I had the wonderful honor of uniting them in marriage. They've been married for 11 years now and have blessed us with two grandsons and one granddaughter. Ain't God good?!

Last but not least, one of my children got it right the first time. My other son married a beautiful Christian girl he met in college at Texas A&M. She came from a fine Christian home and has blessed our family as my other in-laws have done. It's easy to write a book and explain how God has delivered us in desperate times of need, but sometimes we need to reflect on the child that didn't cause us any problems. This young man was that child. As the Doorkeeper of my home, it dawned on me one day that I needed to go into his room and thank him for being such a blessing to raise. He has always had a heart for God and godly things. He now teaches teenagers in his church and is very active as a Christian in the community where he lives. I also had the wonderful opportunity to marry him and his bride, now of 12 years. They have also blessed us with two grandsons!

God is waiting to bless us, but the Doorkeeper must make a decision not to accept the unacceptable and trust God to work His will and His ways in the lives of our family members. God wants to do these kinds of miracles in your home as well, but He won't work through a vessel that's not willing to take a stand when the battle is raging. Give God a chance, and expect Him to do what He says He'll do. He said, "I will never leave you or forsake you!" and "He that honors me I will honor." Those are promises of God, and as the saying goes, you can take that to the bank!

"Do not be bound together with unbelievers, for what partnership have righteousness and lawlessness, or what fellowship has light with darkness?"

—2 Corinthians 6:14

PERSONAL SPIRITUAL INSIGHTS

1. Explain in your own words what it means to you "not to accept the unacceptable."

2. Read 2 Corinthians 6:14. What does God's Word say about being yoked with unbelievers?

It's the Doorkeeper's job to pray and take a stand against your Christian child being married in an unequal yoke. If we fail to take this stand, our children and we will experience heartache upon heartache. Remember, dating turns to marriage! Counsel your children wisely, and keep them in a Christian youth group so they'll have an opportunity to choose the right one the first time! As you and your wife pray for your children's spouse, have faith and believe that God will bring it to pass! Begin Praying NOW!!!

3. What should you do to honor a child who has chosen the right path in his/her life? List the great attributes of all your children.

Now sit down with each of them individually, praising them and praying over them.

A lifetime of joy and blessings will await you and your wife when your children marry Christian mates.

My perspective...

Johnny Swafford

Sonny Guess has been a good friend and business associate of mine for several years now. A little over a year ago, he invited me to go with him on a Spring turkey hunt at his lease in central Texas. On our drive out there, he told me that he had been invited to speak at East Paris Baptist Church, and he asked if I would listen to a tape of his speech. I began to listen to the tape that night, and as I listened, I began to reflect on my own life and view the similarities to his experiences. I thought, *If only I could have heard this message when I was 25 years old and just staring my family!*

I suppose I've listened to that tape 10 times since then, and each time I come away with something else from it. Of course, I can't go back in time and re-do the things I left undone when I was younger, but I began to think how great it would be if every guy could hear this message and learn how to be the Spiritual Doorkeeper of his home. You can imagine how elated I was when Sonny told me God had spoken to him to do this full time and then asked me to serve on the board of directors of the Doorkeepers Ministries!

I truly believe Sonny is ordained by God to bring this message to as many men as possible for as long as he is able to speak. His love for God and his commitment to his Doorkeeper message has been an inspiration to me. Sonny will help any man who is willing to listen, commit himself to be a Doorkeeper, and become a giant roadblock to Satan at the entryway to the door of his home. When you grasp the message of this book, you'll know what I mean.

This Is the Day!

Commitments are made every day, but few are actually kept for very long. The commitment I'm going to ask you to make today is a lifetime commitment. Oh yes, there will be times when you will be weaker than others, but this core commitment will change your family for generations to come! You see, the ministry of the Doorkeeper is just that. It's a ministry! This is a commitment to God to protect your family from the onslaught of evil that's in this world and is trying to permeate every crack and crevice of your home!

As the Doorkeeper, you'll be the husband, father, bread-winner, and spiritual guide in your home. God has given you everything you need to do the many tasks that you're called to do. He has given His precious Holy Spirit to call on night or day to empower you for the task at hand. Learning to listen to the Spirit is something most of us have never been taught. The Holy Spirit speaks to us through our conscience, the Word of God, and wise people that God has placed in our lives to give us instructions and hope. Never do anything throughout the day that you don't ask the Holy Spirit to give you wisdom, guidance, instructions, and peace at that very moment that you are in need. Act immediately upon His instructions, and you'll be totally amazed at what God will do in that situation. Listening to the Holy Spirit on a daily basis is imperative to fulfill your roll as a spiritual Doorkeeper!

You have read this book, and now God wants to know what your choice will be! Will you chose to continue to allow Satan to tear your home apart, or will you confess your weaknesses and failures to the Lord and announce to your wife and family that you have chosen to be the Doorkeeper of your home? If you respond in active obedience, you'll take the responsibility of being the spiritual leader and role model for your wife and children. And you'll take action. You'll clean the garbage out of your home, no matter how difficult this action may be, and you'll see that the love of God and peace will take its place.

God wants to know today what your choice will be! God knew as he looked down through the ages that you would be reading this book today, and you WILL make a choice. There is no maybe! The answer is either "YES" of "NO." As I write this, I pray that you will jump at the chance to be the Doorkeeper of your home!

If you said "yes" to God today, I want you to do something that will help you with your commitment. Go to your local bank and ask for a Sacagawea dollar, a gold-colored coin that's worth one dollar. Every bank should have them. When you get your coin, carry it in you pocket EVERYWHERE you go as a sign of your commitment. When you look on the back of the coin, you'll see an eagle. The Bible says in Isaiah 40:31, "They shall mount their wings as eagles, they shall run and not be weary, they shall walk and not faint." Every time you see the eagle on the coin, you are reminded that the Doorkeeper's job isn't easy, but you are to never tire. Even when the times are tough, don't give up, don't stop, and don't faint. Through the power of the Holy Spirit, you will win the battle!

On the other side of the coin, you'll see a woman and child. This is to remind you of your wife and children. They are the most precious things on this earth that you possess. Someone can take all our material blessings of this world and put them in a pile and burn them, but don't take our families! They are life's greatest possessions! Next to the woman and child on the coin, you'll see a statement of faith that our forefathers believed was important and profound! That statement is, "IN GOD WE TRUST." I hope this statement of faith in God is never taken off our currency in this great United States of America! This statement of faith reminds me that my job as a Doorkeeper isn't easy, but I'm not alone in the battle. God is with me! He has promised He will never leave me nor forsake me, and His promises are true!

Most banks still have some Sacagawea dollars, but since the first printing of this book, the government is no longer making them. If you cannot find one, you can carry anything in your pocket, such as a marble, special coin, special rock, or anything else that reminds you that you are the doorkeeper of your home.

As you carry this coin in your pocket, you'll see it several times a day. The coin will become a conversation piece, but more than that, it will remind you that you have made a permanent commitment to be the Doorkeeper of your home. Your wife will love you! Your children will love you! And most of all, God will be honored and glorified as your church and community see the dramatic transformation that will happen in your home!

As I said at the very first page, this book is not my message! This message came from the Living God! I pray that every fiber in your soul has been touched by the power of God as you've read this book! I know that when the husband and father of the home steps up and accepts his God-given role as the Doorkeeper, revival will break out in America like we experienced in years past! Then and only then will our nation turn back to God and become the nation that He created it to be. ONE NATION UNDER GOD!

TO GOD BE THE GLORY!

PERSONAL SPIRITUAL INSIGHTS

1. As you read through the pages of this book and reflected on the exercises and questions in each chapter, I trust that God's Holy Spirit has convicted you to become the spiritual Doorkeeper of your home!

Will you commit to be the Doorkeeper of your home? Yes or No (circle one).

If yes, please express in writing your commitment to God. (You might need to start with heart-felt repentance for your failures in the past. Thank God for his grace and forgiveness.)

2. Seal your commitment to God by selecting a Sacagawea dollar, special coin, rock, marble, cross, or anything else that reminds you to be the Doorkeeper of your home. Carry it in your pocket, and every time you see it or feel it, you'll be reminded of your commitment. What are some ways remembering this commitment will help you in relationships, responses to difficult circumstances, and opportunities to show love and strength to your family?

Now go, love your wife, clean out your house, instruct and discipline your children in love, and PUT GOD BACK INTO YOUR HOME!!!!!

May the Great God Jehovah bless you as you undertake the huge task of becoming . . .

THE SPIRITUAL DOORKEEPER!!!

My perspective...

Glen Hinshaw

Conviction is a blessing. It's not always about sin. Sometimes it's the leading of the Holy Spirit to do something that will end up honoring God. Either way, it's a good thing. When you listen to Sonny Guess with The Doorkeeper Ministries, you'll get it—conviction that is, from both directions because God is in the message. In fact, God is the message.

As Christians, our desire should be to please, praise and honor God, and the road map is presented to us through conviction from the Holy Spirit. If you want to be a better spiritual leader of your home, a better husband and a better father, take the time to read and apply the principles taught in *The Doorkeeper*. My advice is to be ready to sit down, kneel down and bow down. Conviction is indeed a blessing, and obedience to the Holy Spirit's leading will change our lives.

Thank you, Sonny, for following the leadership of the Holy Spirit and for sharing this message with us.

Sonny and Delores Guess

About the Author

In January of 1965, I married Delores Raney and have been married now 42 years. God gave us three beautiful children and eight delightful grandchildren.

In 1972 God called us into full time music ministry at First Baptist Church of Pearland, Texas. To prepare for this role, we sold all we had, moved to Marshall to attend East Texas Baptist University, and began studying to be what we thought God wanted us to be—a Minister of Music.

From 1972 to 1978, we served the Lord in several Baptist churches in Texas and Florida. In 1978, the Lord changed our ministry and I became the City Business Administrator in Winnsboro, Texas. It was in Winnsboro that the Lord began to teach me great lessons about my family. Experiences with a rebellious child and a child who attempted suicide began to turn my heart toward one of the most neglected things in my life—my family.

As I began to spend hours in Bible Study and prayer, my wife and I learned to rise early in the morning to pray together.

We have seen the power of prayer work in our home. As God worked powerfully in our family to change lives, He began to give me a burden to teach others so they wouldn't have to experience some of the heartaches we went through. God has a beautiful plan for the Christian home!

As God opened doors for this new ministry, I've taught couple's classes in several churches throughout Texas. In the last few years, God has allowed me to teach a mixed class of all ages

My mother-in-law, Rose Mary Raney, and my mother, Marguerite Guess

who want to grow in the Lord. The Holy Spirit is our teacher, and He not only taught us, but He empowered us to minister to many folks as our class has grown. To God be the glory!

As I explain in the first part of this book, I was asked to be a keynote speaker for the men's conference at East Paris Baptist Church in 2005. While I was in my study praying about what

My son David, his wife Denene, and their daughters Brittany, Dakotah, and Mackenzie

My son Michael, his wife Trish, and their sons Caleb and Zachary

My daughter Lisa, her husband Dave, and their sons Tyler and Coby, and their daughter Madison

God would have me speak on, God's Holy Spirit gave me a clear and simple message about men being the Doorkeeper of their homes. In fact, the Holy Spirit gave me this message almost faster than I could write it down. Through the power of the Holy Spirit, I opened my mouth that day and He filled it with a message that came from a life of experiences and scriptural truths concerning a Christian man's role in his home. By His grace, a multitude of lives were changed that day, and that began this ministry—"The Doorkeeper Ministry."

My prayer is that in all we do, Jesus may be lifted up and glorified! I praise God for the power He gives us over the enemy in every area of our lives. God will bless our homes when we live under the spiritual authority He has set up in His Word.

I sincerely hope God will use "The Doorkeeper Ministries" to help men gain a deeper knowledge of their responsibility to protect, defend, teach, and nurture their precious families as they trust the Holy Spirit to equip them to fulfill that role.

About The Doorkeeper Ministries

O ur Mission is to "Bring God's plan to save and protect men and their families, to help them discover the joy of following God's will for their lives."

Sonny is available to speak at your church or conference, to the entire congregation or to the men's ministry. He also is an accomplished musician and will enliven any event with music that inspires people to worship our awesome God.

For more information about scheduling Sonny for an event at your church or to ask any questions you might have about this ministry, contact him at:

Write to: The Doorkeeper Ministries
P.O. Box 3416
Palestine, TX 75802

Phone: (903) 922-3146

Email: SonnyGuess45@gmail.com and put
"Doorkeeper" in the subject line

WHAT PEOPLE ARE SAYING ABOUT DOORKEEPER MINISTRIES

Over the last forty years God has placed in my life many good men who were used to build and strengthen me in Christ. About five years ago, Sonny Guess walked into my life needing help for a family who had lost their home in a fire. Neither of us fully understood the Spirit's leading beyond the family's loss. In the days and months that followed, a friendship developed that brought much joy and freshness into my Christian life and walk. Sonny talked often about a burden God had placed on his heart and how the family of today needs fathers who will be the doorkeepers of their homes.

As I attended the Doorkeeper's Conference at Southside Baptist in Palestine, I realized that the very thing God was preparing in Sonny had come to life. There is not a better man to present these truths to other men than Sonny. He is a man of faith, and he stands on the truth of the Word of God. I wholeheartedly recommend his ministry. I'm convinced that we will hear and see the "mighty works" of God through "The Doorkeepers Ministries."

—Bob Logan, Pastor of Bible Baptist Church,
Tyler, Texas

"What a wonderful experience! God really spoke to my life!" That statement expressed the sentiments of many who attended our men's conference. God is using Sonny Guess to help men understand why so many homes are failing and what they can do to follow the Lord's plan for the home. Thank you, Sonny, for The Doorkeeper Ministries!

—Dr. Steve Holcombe, Pastor Southside Baptist Church, Palestine, Texas

How to Lead a Men's Group or Class Using *The Doorkeeper*

This book is designed for individual study, small groups, and classes. The questions at the end of each chapter stimulate individual reflection so that men wrestle with the specific issues of being the Doorkeeper of their homes, but most men apply truth even more deeply when they talk about the principles with other men. If you are the leader of a men's group, consider using this book as a curriculum for a few weeks. And if you want to start a group, gather some men, challenge them with your vision of what it means to be a Doorkeeper, and schedule a time to meet. Be sure to order enough books so that each man has his own.

The book has nine chapters, but you can tailor the content to fit your group's needs. If you prefer, you can cover two chapters at a time, beginning with the Introduction and Chapter 1, or you can take it a chapter a week. In my experience with men, I've seen the Holy Spirit do some incredible, powerful things in men's lives as they've faced the choices of being God's Doorkeeper, so don't rush the process.

PERSONALIZE THE LESSONS

At least once in each group meeting, tell part of your own story to illustrate a particular point. The men will appreciate your honesty about your failures and the hope you provide when you share how God has changed you and your relationship with your wife and children. Be authentic, and impart hope.

Make the Scriptures come alive. Far too often, we read the Scriptures like it's a phone book, with little or no emotion. Paint a vivid picture for people. Provide insights about the context of the encounters with Christ, and help people sense the emotions of specific people in each scene.

The questions at the end of the chapters will help your group "get real" about the challenges and joys of being a Doorkeeper to your families. Share how you are applying the principles in the chapter, and encourage them to take steps of growth, too.

THREE TYPES OF QUESTIONS

If you have led groups for few years, you already understand the importance of using open questions to stimulate discussion. Three types of questions are *limiting, leading,* and *open.*

— *Limiting questions* focus on an obvious answer, such as, "What does Jesus call himself in John 10:11?" These don't stimulate reflection or discussion. If you want to use questions like this, follow them with thought-provoking open questions.

— *Leading questions* sometimes require the listener to guess what the leader has in mind, such as, "Why did Jesus use the metaphor of a shepherd in John 10?" (He was probably alluding to a passage in Ezekiel, but most people wouldn't know that.) The teacher who asks a leading question has a definite answer in mind. Instead of asking this question, he should teach the point and perhaps ask an open question about the point he has made.

— *Open questions* usually don't have right or wrong answers. They stimulate thinking, and they are far less threatening because the person answering doesn't risk ridicule for being wrong. These questions often begin with "Why do you think…?" or "What are some possible reasons that…?" or "How would you have felt in that situation?"

PREPARATION

As you prepare to teach this material in a group, consider these steps:

1. Carefully and thoughtfully read the book. Make notes, highlight key sections, quotes, or stories, and complete the reflection sections at the end of each chapter. This will familiarize you with the entire scope of the content.

2. As you prepare for each lesson, read the corresponding chapter again and make additional notes.

3. Tailor the amount of content to the time allotted. You

may not have time to cover all the questions in great detail, so pick the ones that are most pertinent and make sure to provide enough time for those.

4. Add your own stories to personalize the message and add impact.

5. Before and during your preparation, ask God to give you wisdom, clarity, and power. Trust Him to use your group to change people's lives.

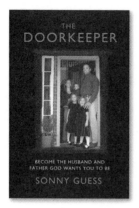

The Doorkeeper is designed to help men and men's groups experience God's purpose, pardon, and power as the Doorkeepers of their homes. Order copies for your friends, your staff or leadership team, or your men's group. Use the discussion questions at the end of each chapter to stimulate interaction, gain insights, and make application of the principles in the book.

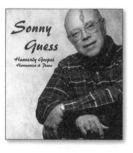

"Heavenly Gospel" is an inspiring CD that showcases Sonny's talent on the harmonica and piano. The songs are instrumentals recorded at Daywind Music in Hendersonville, Tennessee.

SONNY'S NEW BOOK!

In *Then It Happened!*, Sonny tells inspiring, touching—and often humorous—stories of his experiences of letting the Holy Spirit lead him and use him to touch the lives of others.

FOR MORE COPIES OF THE BOOK AND THE CD...

Email:	SonnyGuess45@gmail.com and put "Doorkeeper" in the subject line
Call:	(903) 922-3146
Write to:	The Doorkeeper Ministries
	P.O. Box 3416
	Palestine, TX 75802

SPREAD THE WORD

GOD IS USING THIS BOOK IN POWERFUL WAYS. IF YOU WOULD LIKE TO MAKE A TAX-DEDUCTIBLE DONATION TO HELP DISTRIBUTE COPIES OF THIS BOOK, SEND A CHECK PAYABLE TO THE DOORKEEPER MINISTRIES TO:

> The Doorkeeper Ministries
> P.O. Box 3416
> Palestine, TX 75802

WE WANT TO HEAR FROM YOU!

I hope God has used the message of this book to encourage you and help you become the husband and father God wants you to be. We all face big challenges, and we need to hear how others are meeting those challenges. I want to invite you to send me an email and tell me your story of courageous steps you've taken to become the doorkeeper of your home. You can share as much or as little as you prefer (and you can change names and details to protect anonymity). You can also upload a picture of you and your family with your story.

Will you share your heart with others to encourage them? I hope you will. Email me at: **SonnyGuess45@gmail.com**